FLEX YOUR WRITING MUSCLE

365 WRITING PROMPTS

A MONTH-BY-MONTH GUIDE

By

Jan Fishler

Copyright © 2015 by Jan Fishler

ISBN:978-0-9826723-2-7

All rights reserved. No part of this publication may be reproduced, distributed, or transmitted in any form or by any means, including photocopying, recording, or other electronic or mechanical methods, without the prior written permission of the publisher, except in the case of brief quotations embodied in critical reviews and certain other noncommercial uses permitted by copyright law. For permission requests, write to the publisher, addressed "Attention: Permissions Coordinator," at the address below. You can also contact the publisher at 530-264-5105.

Tin Cat Media
10844 Thomas Dr.
Nevada City, CA 95959

Quantity sales. Special discounts are available on quantity purchases by corporations, associations, and others. For details, contact the publisher at the address above.

Printed in the United States of America

For writers who enjoy having a daily jump-start

About Jan

Jan Fishler is the author of *Searching for Jane, Finding Myself (An Adoption Memoir)*, available at Amazon.com, and the producer of *The Path to Publication* DVD series, featuring such well-known authors as Amy Tan, Anne Lamott, Janet Fitch, and Mark Childress. She is also the creator and presenter of Write Your Story workshops where she teaches a growth-oriented process for those wanting to leave a legacy or live a better life. Recently, Jan published the eBook, *PTSD: Lessons from Vietnam*, based on a series of articles previously published in *Vietnow National Magazine*. She is the co-author of *Cooking Up a Plan: Turn Your Novel Idea Into a Book*. She lives in the foothills of the Sierra Nevada.

Find out more about Jan and her work at **www.janfishler.com.**

Why Prompts

At the beginning of 2014, a friend challenged me to post on my blog for 365 days in a row. Of course, I accepted without thinking about what the content might be. I wanted to post something that would be useful to my visitors without taking up too much of my time. That's when the idea of posting writing prompts occurred to me. Prompts are an excellent way to flex your writing muscle and jump-start your day. They can jog memories, help you tap into a part of your subconscious, and get you started when you're suffering from procrastination, writer's block, or the dreaded white page. Prompts that "speak" to you can become the beginning of a new project or launch a series of blog posts. Some are simply cathartic or therapeutic while others might help you develop characters for a short story or novel. I encourage you to give them a try and see what effect they have on your writing.

How it Works

In my *Write Your Story* workshops, I encourage people to begin their day by writing for five minutes. I've been doing this for years now with varying outcomes. I keep a notebook by my bed and begin my writing longhand. Sometimes, I'm writing a dream fragment or putting items on a to-do list, but most often I end up writing for thirty minutes or so about what is going on in my life or about a project I'm working on. The morning writing clears my mind and generally helps me set my intention for the day. In fact, many of the prompts in this book were a result of writing longhand in my notebook. Over the years, morning writing has also helped me come up with viable solutions to many of life's little problems.

Month-by-Month

If you're not accustomed to writing first thing in the morning, or if you'd like to try something new, I encourage you to move through the prompts month by month, in order. If a prompt doesn't "speak" to you, then by all means skip it. Each month has a focus or theme designed to provide insight in a particular area. Whether you use the prompts for personal growth, for character development, or a combination of both is entirely up to you. As you write, keep in mind that prompts are merely a nudge of encouragement. Some of them will be highly stimulating and motivate you to beyond your expectations while others will simply be fun.

To get the most out of this book, read the prompt, set a timer for five minutes, put your pen on the page or your hands on the keyboard, set judgment aside, and see what you can get down on the page. After five minutes you can decide whether you'll continue with the content you have or move on to something else.

JANUARY

January is a good time to think about your goals and set your intention for the coming year. Rather than make resolutions that will undoubtedly be broken, the prompts for this month are simply a way to get you thinking about the coming year and what you hope to accomplish. January is also a good time to take stock of your attitudes and think about what is and is not working for you. Perhaps your priorities have changed and you need to adjust your schedule and lifestyle to match. Maybe you've changed jobs, moved, gotten married or divorced. What about money? Do you have enough? How can you get more? The prompts for January will help you take stock of your current situation and assess where you are, where you want to go, and how you might get there.

Write about your goals.

Write at least three personal and three professional goals for this year. Why are these goals important to you?

Write about what stops you.

Look at the goals you have written. What might prevent you from reaching them? What are the ways you have sabotaged your efforts in the past? How will you prevent this from happening in the future?

Write about your main priority.

What is the most important goal for this year? Why is this a priority? How will accomplishing this goal make you feel?

Write about the person you can count on.

Who is the one person you can count on to help you meet your most important goal? What qualities, traits, and attributes allow you to rely on him or her? If you don't have someone like this in your life, create a fictionalized character who would be your most supportive friend and confidant.

Write about attributes.

What traits do you need to cultivate to be more successful? What beliefs, thoughts, and habits would help you achieve your goals?

Write about changing yourself.

If you could change one thing about yourself what would it be? How would that change impact your personal and professional life? What prevents you from changing?

Write about changing another.

What one thing would you like to change about your spouse, significant other, your best friend, boss, or other important person in your life?

Write about money.

Do you believe that "money makes the world go 'round?" What does money mean to you? What role does it play in your life?

Write about your attitude about money.

How do your attitudes about money shape or influence your life? If you don't have enough money, how can you make more?

Write about winning money.

Imagine winning a million dollars. What would you do with it? How would it feel to win a lot of money?

Write about problems with money.

Is money the "root of all evil?" Explain.

Write about having no money.

Write about someone (real or imagined) who is flat broke. How did they get that way? What will they do about it?

Write about the richest person you know.

Compare the richest person you know to the poorest person you have known. What values do they have in common? What attributes if any do they share?

Write about money and happiness.

Does money buy happiness? Why or why not.

Write about the one thing you can count on.

Describe the person or situation in detail even if this person is yourself.

Write about having magical powers.

If you had magical powers, who would you make disappear and why?

Write about your perfect day.

Where would you be, who would you be with, what would you be doing? Has this ever happened?

Write about the future.

What would you like to be doing in five years? How does your life look? Where are you living? What are you doing?

Write about something you are afraid to do.

Fear is the acronym for False Expectations Appearing Real. What would your life be like if you pushed FEAR aside?

Write about inspiration.

In honor of Martin Luther King Jr. day, write about someone (living or dead) who inspires you.

Write a letter.

Write a letter to someone with whom you have unfinished business. Speak your truth. Say everything you wish they would hear. Shred the letter.

Write about the letter.

Write about how yesterday's letter-writing experience made you feel.

Write about something you need to sell or donate.

Do you hold on to people and things that no longer serve you? What's stopping you from letting them go?

Write about your best attribute.

Celebrate your uniqueness and what makes you special.

Write about someone in your life who drives you crazy.

What does this person look like? How old are they? What do they do or say that gets on your nerves? Why do you think that is the case?

Write about your temperament.

Are you an optimist or a pessimist? Why? What experiences have made you who you are today?

Write about lies.

When was the last time you lied? Write about the biggest lie you've ever told. Why do you lie?

Write about avoidance.

What people or situations do you avoid? Why?

Write about time.

If you could time-travel, where would you go? What would you do there? How long would you stay?

Write about your legacy.

100 years from now, how would you like to be remembered? What legacy would you like to leave behind?

Revise your goals.

Go back to January 1 and review the goals you wrote for the year. Make necessary revisions.

FEBRUARY

February prompts are about feelings. From love to hate, writers need to consider our own feelings as well as those of the characters we are developing. Whether we are aware of it or not, our feelings motivate our actions. If your character is filled with sadness and grief, he will behave differently than someone who is full of lust or hate. Often, we pay no attention to our feelings and either ignore them or anesthetize ourselves so that we don't have to feel them. Knowing more about your own feelings will help you develop yourself as a writer as well as the characters you write about.

Write about feelings.

What feelings are you currently hiding? Why are you keeping these feelings to yourself? What do you believe would happen if you expressed one or more of them?

Write about your happiest memory.

When did it happen? Who was with you? Why did this person, place or thing make you happy? How long did the happy feeling last? Does just thinking about this memory make you happy? Are you generally a happy person? Why or why not.

Write about your shadow.

We all have a shadow side, but most of us would prefer to keep it tucked away, out of sight. Give your shadow a name and write about it as if you were an outside observer. Create a character sketch based on this shadow.

Write about relief.

We all have times when we feel relieved about an outcome or experience, something that did or did not come to pass. When was the last time you "breathed a sigh of relief?" When did you feel comfortable again after worrying about something?

Write about ecstasy.

No, I'm not talking about 34-methylenedioxy-methamphetamine, but don't let me stop you if that's where you want to go with this. I'm more interested in having you write about a time you experienced delight, bliss, or elation that wasn't drug-induced. What were you doing? Who was with you? How long did the "high" last? When thinking about the experience, can you recreate the feeing?

Write about your worst nightmare.

What is the absolutely worst thing that could happen to you? Now, write a fictionalized scene—a page or so, and have that happen to a character. Does your character find their way out of the dilemma? If so, how? If not, what happens next? Write about the consequences.

Write about surprise.

Complete the following sentence: Nothing could surprise me more than _____.
Explain why this is so. What would you do if this actually happened? What could you do to make it happen?

Write about anger.

What person, place, or thing fills you with the most anger? Why is this so? Do you believe that these thoughts and feelings impact your health? What color do you associate with anger? Write a poem about that color.

Write about regret.

Use the following quote by author Libba Bray to get you started. "We all do things we desperately wish we could undo. Those regrets just become part of who we are, along with everything else. To spend time trying to change that, well, it's like chasing clouds." What do you desperately wish you could undo? How would your life be different if this thing was undone?

Write about relief.

When was the last time you felt relieved? What were the circumstances that caused you to feel distress prior to feeling relief?

Write about envy.

Who or what do you envy? Psychologists believe envy is one of the main causes of unhappiness. Do you think this is true? Why do you think Shakespeare called jealousy the "green-eyed monster?" How do feelings of envy affect your life?

Write about repulsion.

Not the happiest of topics, but there are times when a person or situation is, well, simply disgusting. Recall the details of this event. Tap into your inner comedian and write about it in a way that makes you (and your readers) laugh.

Write about hate.

Hate is such a strong feeling that it can run our lives if we let it. Today, write about a person, place, food, concept, or idea that you absolutely hate. Explain when this feeling began, why it has such a grip on you, and if or when you would be willing to let it go.

Write about love.

In honor of Valentine's Day, it only makes sense to write about love and what the word means to you. Have you loved and lost? Are you in love? Do you wish you were in love? What do you love most? Write about whatever comes up without judgment or blame.

Write about being amazed.

When was the last time you were amazed? Was it something you witnessed, read, heard, did? Explain why it was so amazing? Or write about the person who you find most amazing. What have they done or are they doing that is so astonishing?

Write about something you dread.

We all avoid doing various tasks, or being around certain people. What is the one thing that fills you with the most anxiety? Snakes? Public Speaking? Heights? Write a couple of paragraphs about how and why you avoid these situations.

Write about something you've been avoiding.

Why aren't you doing it? What would happen if you never did it? What would happen if you stopped and did it right now? Write about why you avoid this particular thing and how this avoidance makes you feel.

Write about shame.

What are your deepest, darkest thoughts and feelings? Describe a situation where you felt shame. Write without stopping. Then, shred or burn what you've written. Now, doesn't that feel better?

Write a letter of apology.

The letter can be written to someone who is living or dead. This is an opportunity to say everything you "should" say or "should" have said. Be clear, concise, honest and forthright.

Only send the letter if you believe it will improve your relationship.

Rewrite history.

Take a scene from your life and give it the happy ending you wish it had. Include how you felt before and how the new ending makes you feel. What did you learn from rewriting history?

Write about road rage.

We've all witnessed or experienced road rage at one time or another. What do other drivers do to piss you off? Why do you become so annoyed? Pick a road rage situation and write a scene that occurred before the person got into their car.

Write about lust.

Do you lust after chocolate, an expensive pair of boots or leather jacket, your neighbor's husband or wife, or your best friend's salary? Perhaps you lust for power? Whatever it is, imagine you have this particular thing and write about how you got it and how it feels having it.

Write about grief.

What makes you sad? Have you lost a pet, child, parent, sibling, lover, job, or home? Grief can fill our hearts and make moving forward seem impossible. Give your sadness and grief color and shape and write about it as if you're describing a painting.

Write about joy.

What person, place, thing, or situation brings you the most joy? What do you like to do when you are feeling joyful? Write about how you can bring more joy into your life.

Write about feeling nervous.

When was the last time you felt nervous? Where were you? What were you doing? What goes on physiologically when you are nervous? What do you think about?

Write about judgment.

Do you judge other people? What do you judge about them—their appearance, financial or employment status, religion or belief system? How does judging others make you feel?

Write about criticism.

Think back to your childhood. Were you criticized by a parent or teacher? What did they say about you? Did you believe them then? Do you believe them now? How has this criticism affected your life?

Write about your current state of being.

What emotion are you feeling right now? Love, joy, surprise, anger, sadness, disgust, fear? Write about how you are feeling today or the emotion you feel most often. Does this feeling drive your actions? If so, how?

MARCH

In March, while the winds are blowing, I thought it would be interesting to think about various themes that play out in our lives or the lives of our fictional characters. For example, such universal ideas as injustice, isolation, and good versus bad, are universal concepts that have been repeated throughout history. Themes show up in a variety of ways. They can be life's lessons, repetitive patterns, or insights we have about ourselves and others. Throughout the month of March, see how you resonate with the various prompts and see if you can discover themes that affect your life and the life of your characters.

Write about life themes.

A theme is a message that stretches through a book or novel, or a period of time. What is the major theme that has played out in your life?

Write about survival.

The will to survive is a popular theme in literature. Write about how this theme has played out in your life or in the life of someone you know. What characteristics does someone need to have the will to survive?

Write about fear of failure or success.

Fear of failure is a common theme. Fear of success is less common, but it can also sabotage our efforts. Are you or is your character afraid to fail or succeed? Write about the incident that may have triggered this fear.

Write about the need to escape.

Many films are about the necessity or the need to escape. Have you ever been in a situation that made you feel trapped? Perhaps you have been held hostage. Write about that experience.

Write about loss of innocence.

When and how did you lose your innocence? Who was involved? Where did it happen? Write about it in the third person, as if it happened to one of your characters.

Write about family.

Family can be a blessing and a curse. Which was your family? Has it made you stronger or sent you running to therapy? List five ways your family has affect you and your life. Pick the most important one and write about it in detail.

Write about chaos versus order.

Some people thrive on order and others are quite content to live with chaos. In which camp do you reside? Write a scene where someone enters and upends your comfort zone, turning order into chaos or vice versa.

Write about simplicity.

Life often gets complicated and what we want most is simplicity. Write a scene about a complication in your life or in the life of a fictional character. Write that scene without the complication. Which scene is more interesting? Is there beauty in simplicity or is it boring?

Write about daylight saving time.

Write a scene or a short story about daylight saving time. If Daylight is a person, what does she look like? Does she have super powers and if so, what are they? Why did Time need to be saved? Make up something wild and crazy. Submit it to a fiction-writing contest.

Write about everlasting love.

Do you believe in everlasting love? What about love at first sight? Write a scene where two strangers meet and instantaneously fall in love.

Write about death.

We're all going to die, but many people don't like to talk or think about it. Imagine an ideal death, then write a scene where the ideal death happens to one of your characters. You define ideal.

Write about man or woman versus nature.

Imagine you are lost in the wilderness and your cell phone is dead. A winter storm is coming in and it's freezing cold. You desperately want to live, but are afraid help won't come in time. Write at least 800 words about this situation. What attributes do you need to survive this ordeal, assuming you survive?

Write about luck.

Some people think the number 13 is unlucky. Has this number played a role in your life? Was it lucky or unlucky?

Is superstition a character flaw or a useful attribute? Write a scene where Lady Luck either appears to save the day or disappears.

Write about aging, fading beauty.

For women in particular, the loss of their looks can be devastating. Imagine what it would be like to be a "beauty queen" who is stuck in the past or an action figure who loses his or her super powers. Write dialogue about what they are thinking and what they do after being rejected for a part in a movie.

Write about injustice.

There is so much injustice in the world that it's difficult to focus on one cause. Write a Letter to the Editor about an injustice that is occurring in your community. Be sure to include a solution to the problem. Send the letter and see what happens.

Write about wealth.

Wealth is power. It can also be a destructive force or used for good. Write about someone who wins the lottery and wants to use the money to harm an adversary. Include in the story someone who tries to change his or her mind.

Write about identity crisis.

Imagine that you are not who you think you are, that everything you have been told about your identity is a lie, and that instead of being human, you are part of an alien species that has landed on earth. Your mission is to "wake up" humanity. Write a scene where you discover your true destiny.

Write about good and bad.

First, write about something good that is going on in your life or in your community, then write about something bad that is going on in your life or community and what you can do about it. Perhaps you need to adjust your thinking. Maybe you need to get involved.

Write about how life is not fair.

Life is not fair. Or is it? Imagine a scene where someone is falsely accused of a crime and injustice is served. Write about the circumstances. What is the outcome?

Write about male and female roles.

What role and responsibility have you taken on because you are either male or female? What would happen if you no longer accepted this role? Write a scene about how different life would be.

Write about rebirth.

Spring can be a metaphor for rebirth. Create a character who wakes up and discovers he or she has been reborn with psychic powers. Write a scene where this character tries out his or her new skills.

Write about temptation.

We are all tempted by something. For some it's as benign as binging on chocolate. Others are enticed by drugs, alcohol, or sex. Write about a situation (real or imagined) where someone can no longer control an urge.

Write about coming of age.

We've all had to grow up. For some, growing up was painful, and for others childhood was blissful. Which childhood situation creates better people and consequently better characters? Write a scene from your childhood that has contributed to who you are today.

Write about power and immortality.

If you had power and were also immortal, what would be your priority? What would you do to change the world and make it a better place? Describe in detail the actions you would take.

Write about materialism.

If you had an unlimited supply of money, what would you buy? How much would you give away? How does being around materialist people make you feel? If you are materialistic, what do you think caused you to be that way?

Write about reunion.

Write a scene where two people who haven't seen one another in a long time come together. What events led up to this reunion? How did this reunion affect the people who were involved? Why had they been separated? What happens now that they have been reunited?

Write about nonverbal communication.

Much of what we understand about people comes from what they do, not what they say. Write a scene where two people are angry with one another, but neither is willing to say a word. Be sure to include the location of the scene and the senses: touch, taste, sight, sound, and smell.

Write about passing judgment.

It's easy to judge others, but often the people we judge have a different story once we get to know them. Write about a situation where you erroneously passed judgment. Include how you felt when you discovered the truth.

Write about marriage.

Imagine being married for 25 years and discovering that your spouse has been unfaithful for many of them. Many people would be angry and upset or blame themselves. There are other options. Make this common situation interesting by coming up with an atypical reaction to this discovery.

Write about tradition.

Write about a family tradition that you have carried on or plan on continuing. Write about a family tradition that drives you crazy. Are traditions important or not?

Write about facing reality.

So often the reality of a situation is so painful that we refuse to face it. Write about a situation where you (or your character) refuse to face reality. What are you avoiding? Why is he or she afraid to face the truth of a particular situation?

APRIL

April, traditionally a rainy month, is a good time to contemplate the wisdom we all have within us. The writing prompts for this month are inspired by Native American teachings found in, *Medicine Cards* and *Sacred Path Cards* by Jamie Sams. Read the prompt and then spend at least five minutes writing your response to the question or commentary. If the prompt inspires you, keep writing.

Write about fertility.

Are you as fertile or prolific in your writing (or in your life) as you would like to be? Write about what it would take for you to become more fertile with your words, your work, your relationships. What seeds need to be planted?

Write about action.

Whatever we resist persists. What have you been ignoring? What would happen if you finally took action? Write about that outcome.

Write about a nightmare

What keeps you up at night? What inner conflict has become a nightmare? Write your way into a better situation.

Write about release.

What are you holding onto that you no longer need? How would you feel if you finally let it go? Write about releasing the attitude, belief, person, situation, etc., that just needs to go.

Write about reflections.

What we project into the world often comes back at us through the behaviors of others. If you stopped a certain behavior (you know the one), what affect would it have on the people around you? Write a scene about this.

Write about passion.

What motivates you? Write about your passion and your deepest desire. Who would you be if nothing was stopping you? Give this passionate character a name and describe him or her in detail.

Write about spontaneity.

When was the last time you did something spontaneously? Did it work for you? Write about what prevents you from being more spontaneous and what (if anything) you can do to bring more spontaneity into your life.

Write about lessons.

What has been your greatest lesson? Who taught it to you? Write about the lesson you learned or are still learning.

Write about confrontation.

Write about something you have been putting off and need to confront. Why have you not dealt with this challenge? What are you afraid of?

Write about discipline.

Are you a disciplined person or do you tend to spin out of control? Maybe you're somewhere in the middle. Write about a situation where you "should" have had more discipline. What were the consequences?

Write about rhythm.

Are you a people-pleaser or do you walk to the rhythm of your own drum? What circumstances made you the way you are?

Write about death and rebirth.

Imagine you have died and can come back as anything or anyone you choose. Who or what would you be and why?

Write about decisions.

Write about the decisions you aren't making. Then, write about how your life would be if you stood up for yourself. How would this shift make you feel?

Write about victory.

Have you ever experienced victory after a long defeat? Write about the circumstances leading up to the win. If you've never had this experience, write about someone you know who has.

Write about self-expression.

What are the ways you express yourself? What do your clothes, hairstyle, car, pets, employment, etc., say about who you are? Is this an accurate representation of the *real* you?

Write about worry.

What do you worry about? Write about all of your concerns, then imagine how life would be if you stopped thinking about these things for a minute, an hour, a day or for the rest of your life.

Write about humor.

What is the funniest thing that ever happened to you or a character in a movie or book? How can you bring more humor into your life?

Write about opinions.

Whether we express them or not, we all have opinions. Write about an opinion you have that you are afraid to express. What prevents you from speaking the truth about this topic? What could happen if you did?

Write about unity.

Are there aspects of your life that prevent you from feeling connected to others? How can you create more unity – within yourself, your family, your community and the world?

Write about camouflage.

If you could be a fly on the wall, where would you go? What would you want to see and hear? What would you observe? What would you do with this information?

Write about connection.

Do you feel connected or disconnected to yourself, friends, family, and to the earth? If you could connect with anyone who would it be? Why? What would you talk about? What would you do?

Write about wisdom.

What life lessons have helped you grow? How have these difficult situations shaped your life? Do you honor your inner-knowing or do you pretend you don't hear the quiet whispers?

Write about change.

Do you resist change or go with the flow? If money was not an issue, what would you change about your life? How can you adjust your thinking to make your life better (easier, more fun)?

Write about joy.

What fills your heart with joy? What prevents you from being more joyful? Write about steps you can take to bring more joy into your life?

Write about seeking.

Create a character who is a "seeker." What is he or she looking for? Imagine that this person goes on a Vision Quest – a silent retreat in nature to seek direction in life. Write about their experience.

Write about attitude.

Pick an attitude you have about a person, place, or thing and write about it from the opposite point of view. For example, if you dislike your boss or neighbor, imagine a scene where your attitude has shifted and you work together on a project. Try the converse: imagine hating your lover or best friend.

Write about introspection.

Spend a few moments sitting quietly. See what comes up in your "monkey mind." Watch your thoughts. Grab one and write about it.

Write about truth and lies.

What lies do you tell yourself and others? What prevents you from speaking the truth? Write about a situation where you decide to speak your truth and say what needs to be said. Create an ideal outcome.

Write about fear.

Make a list of everything you fear. Pick the worst one and write your way out of the situation.

Write about new abilities.

What skills and knowledge would enhance your life? How exactly would these abilities affect your present and future circumstances?

MAY

This month I thought it would be fun to use quotes for inspiration. Whether you agree or disagree, quotes generally make us think about a particular aspect of life—either our own circumstances or those of a character we are writing about. This month, see how a particular quote affects you and how you choose to respond. As always, write for at least five minutes. Keep in mind, the prompts can apply to you personally, or to one of your characters.

Write about something that touches your heart and how it makes you feel.

The best and most beautiful things in the world cannot be seen or even touched - they must be felt with the heart.
~Helen Keller

What are you feeling in your heart? Is it beautiful or is it causing you pain?

Write about suffering.

I hated every minute of training, but I said, 'Don't quit. Suffer now and live the rest of your life as a champion.
~Muhammad Ali

Think about a time or situation when you suffered. Did suffering make you a better person?

Write about the present.

Your present circumstances don't determine where you can go; they merely determine where you start. ~Nido Qubein

Pick an aspect of daily life and use it to launch a short story or poem.

Write about taking charge.

If you don't design your own life plan, chances are you'll fall into someone else's plan. And guess what they have planned for you? Not much. ~Jim Rohn

Write about a time when you were not in charge of your own life. How did this experience make you feel? What did you do or what could you do to change it?

Write about motivation.

A creative man is motivated by the desire to achieve, not by the desire to beat others. ~Ayn Rand

Write about what motivates you. Is it the desire to achieve or the desire to beat others? Be honest.

Write about actions.

Do you want to know who you are? Don't ask. Act! Action will delineate and define you. ~Thomas Jefferson

What actions have you taken that define you from others in the crowd? If you haven't taken action, write about what is stopping you.

Write about attitude.

There is little difference in people, but that little difference makes a big difference. That little difference is attitude. The

big difference is whether it is positive or negative. ~Robert Collier

Does your attitude help or hinder your progress? Write about a situation where an attitude adjustment could be helpful.

Write about love.

I have found the paradox that if you love until it hurts, there can be no more hurt, only more love. ~Mother Teresa

What or who have you loved until it hurts? Do you agree or disagree with Mother Teresa?

Write about simplicity.

Life is really simple, but we insist on making it complicated. ~Confucius

How is your life more complicated than it needs to be? Who would you (or your character) be without the drama?

Write about necessity.

I was born with music inside me. Music was one of my parts. Like my ribs, my kidneys, my liver, my heart. Like my blood. It was a force already within me when I arrived on the scene. It was a necessity for me-like food or water. ~Ray Charles

What in your life is a necessity? What would you do if you lost that one important thing?

Write about six minutes.

If my doctor told me I had only six minutes to live, I wouldn't brood. I'd type a little faster. ~Isaac Asimov

What would you do if you had only six minutes to live? Write about your final thoughts.

Write about something important.

The love of family and the admiration of friends is much more important than wealth and privilege. ~Charles Kuralt

Do you agree or disagree with this statement? What is the most important thing in your life?

Write about a secret.

If you cannot get rid of the family skeleton, you may as well make it dance. ~George Bernard Shaw

Write about the skeleton in your family closet. What would happen if everyone knew about it?

Write an untold story.

There is no greater agony than bearing an untold story inside you. ~Maya Angelou

There's no time like the present to begin writing that untold story. What will it take to start writing yours?

Write about friendship.

A friend is someone who gives you total freedom to be yourself. ~Jim Morrison

Write about that friend. If you don't have anyone like that in your life, then create a character who gives you total freedom to be yourself.

Write about survival.

I don't measure a man's success by how high he climbs but how high he bounces when he hits bottom. ~George S. Patton

Write about your darkest hour and what you did to make a comeback or to survive the experience.

Write about need.

After nourishment, shelter and companionship, stories are the thing we need most in the world. ~Philip Pullman

What story do you need to be writing? Start writing it!

Write about education.

It is a thousand times better to have common sense without education than to have education without common sense. ~Robert Green Ingersoll

When has your education failed you? When has common sense saved the day?

Write about writing.

The first draft of anything is shit. ~Ernest Hemingway

Go look at a first draft of something you've written and see what you can do to make it better.

Write about rules.

If I'd observed all the rules, I'd never have got anywhere. ~Marilyn Monroe

What rules have you broken? What did breaking the rules get you?

Write about learning.

By three methods we may learn wisdom: First, by reflection, which is noblest; second, by imitation, which is easiest; and third by experience, which is the bitterest. ~Confucius

Write about your biggest life's lesson. Include how you felt at the time and what you have learned since.

Write about writing.

I write to give myself strength. I write to be the characters that I am not. I write to explore all the things I'm afraid of. ~Joss Whedon

Why do you write? What is the benefit? What has writing helped you conquer or overcome?

Write about conflict.

Don't forget what I discovered that over ninety percent of all national deficits from 1921 to 1939 were caused by payments for past, present, and future wars. ~Franklin D. Roosevelt

Do you believe in war as a way to resolve differences and conflict? Are there alternatives? Explain your belief.

Write about convictions.

And by the way, everything in life is writable about if you have the outgoing guts to do it, and the imagination to improvise. The worst enemy to creativity is self-doubt. ~Sylvia Plath

Do you have the guts to stand by your convictions or are you filled with self-doubt? What topic are you afraid to write about? Go ahead and write about it.

Write about flow.

Start writing, no matter what. The water does not flow until the faucet is turned on. ~Louis L'Amour

Close your eyes, take three slow, deep breaths, put your hands on the keyboard and start writing nonstop about whatever is on your mind. Write this way, without editing as you go for as long as you can.

Write about waiting.

Don't wait. The time will never be just right. ~Napoleon Hill

Write about whatever it is you've been waiting for. Write a scene where that thing has materialized.

Write about risk.

Everything you've ever wanted is on the other side of fear. ~George Addair

Explain how fear thwarts your efforts. What is the worst that could happen if you took that risk?

Write about what you have.

Do what you can, where you are, with what you have. ~Teddy Roosevelt

Does this statement apply to anything in your life? Do you use what you have or are you waiting for something better?

Write about purpose.

The purpose of our lives is to be happy. ~Dalai Lama

Write about the people, places, things, or circumstances that make you happy. If you're not happy, write about what you can do to change your situation.

Write about acquisitions.

The price of anything is the amount of life you exchange for it. ~Henry David Thoreau

What does this quote mean to you? Have you paid too high a price for some of your acquisitions? What did you purchase that you wish you could return?

Write about passion.

Music is my religion. ~Jimi Hendrix

What is your passion? Do you make enough time to follow your bliss?

JUNE

The prompts for June are based on *The Book of Runes* by Ralph Blum. Runes were used by Vikings to point their attention towards hidden fears and motivations that could shape their future. When used as oracles, Runes can mirror our subconscious process and provide helpful insights. As writing prompts, Runes can direct our attention to such concepts as strength, fertility, and possessions. I hope you have fun with this and perhaps gain some insight that will help you develop your characters or improve the quality of your own life.

Write about wellbeing.

What do you require for your wellbeing? Possessions, better health, more love, improved communications with family and friends? Or perhaps you have enjoyed good fortune. Write about the possessions that make you appreciate your life.

Write about retreat.

There are times when it's a good idea to take a break from someone or something and contemplate other options. Write about where you would go, how long you would stay, and what you would do (or not do) while you were away. How would you like life to be upon your return?

Write about protection.

How do you protect yourself from outside influences? If you don't feel protected, what could you do to feel more safe and secure? Write about a time when you let down your guard and suffered the consequences for being too open.

Write about movement.

There are areas in everyone's life that could stand some change or improvement. Write about a current situation that can benefit from a shift in attitude or a physical change. Be sure to include the steps required to actually make this happen.

Write about opening.

Write about a part of your life that has been or is shrouded in darkness. What events occurred to create this situation? What clarity have you gained from this situation? How can you or will you move toward the light in the future?

Write about flow.

Write about a time in your life when good things effortlessly happened and your intuition was at an all-time high. How long did the spell last? What broke it? What could you do to make it return? How could it be sustained?

Write about strength.

When it is time to grow and change, we often have to draw upon our inner strength. Write about the inner resources that allow you to move forward in life or a time when you suffered a loss that turned out to be an opportunity for transformation.

Write about awareness.

What limitations prevent you from walking through the gate (a metaphor for greater awareness) and entering a place of greater knowledge and insight? Write your way out of your current belief system or situation and experience the other side.

Write about tests.

What life experiences have you gone through that tested you in some way, and what clarity did you earn as a result of a particular trial? Pick one of those tests and write about who you were before and who you have become. How could you share your insight with others?

Write about desire.

What is your innermost desire, the part of you no one knows? Take time to write a detailed scene where you accomplish this goal? What does it take to break through the real and imagined barriers? What could you do to change the course of your life and make this dream a reality?

Write about the ideal.

Imagine your ideal day. Where would you be, what would you be doing, who would be with you, what would you bring along? Write about that day in exquisite detail. Compare how you feel before the day started and how you feel afterward.

Write about standing still.

Write about a time when you have been powerless to do anything about a situation. What had to be put on hold and for how long? Did you harbor resentment about these circumstances? Perhaps you're still at a standstill.

Write about persistence.

What is persisting because of your resistance? What could you do to affect the desired change? In an effort to create a better understanding of your situation, write a dialogue between you and your higher self. Include a solution for removing all resistance.

Write about yourself.

Contemplate the words of Hamlet, "To thine own self be true." Write about a time when you have not been true to yourself. Why the charade? Develop a character who is your true self. What can this character do that you can't? How can you be more like this character?

Write about destiny.

What is your ultimate destiny? What fears prevent you from achieving your ultimate potential? Imagine a world where these fears no longer exist. Describe the path you will follow to get to where you know you should be. Write about the allies who help you along the way and the various obstacles you circumvent or overcome.

Write about partnership.

Have you ever had a great partnership? Even if you haven't, you can write about the qualities your ideal business or marriage partner would have. Describe this person in detail paying particular attention to their assets and talents, how they complement you, and what you will accomplish together that you are unable to accomplish on your own.

Write about fertility.

What rut, habit, cultural pattern, or relationship needs to go for you to have a new beginning? Write about the situation that has been holding you back and what you can do to sow seeds in fertile ground. Describe in detail what will bloom in your garden.

Write about fighting.

What battles are you fighting? Are you winning or losing? What would you have to do to move toward peace? Write a scene where you use your warrior energy to create a positive outcome.

Write about harvest.

What goals have you set that require you to persevere? Write about how you have been able to stay the course. What harvest did you reap or do you hope to reap? If you were unable to stick with the task at hand, write about the obstacles you were unable to overcome.

Write about wholeness.

What do you need to do to regenerate and recharge your energy? How do you manage to keep your spirits up when adversity occurs? Write about a situation when "Let go and let God" was the only option.

Write about disruption.

Think of what you covet most and then imagine it being taken away from you by natural forces such as a tornado, earthquake, or hurricane. Create a scene where you watch the disruption that is entirely out of your control.

Write about misfortune.

Write about the part of you that attracts misfortune. What would happen if those impulses were never controlled? Demonstrate the power of the shadow in a scene.

Write about patience.

When in your life has it made sense to be patient? Were you patient enough or did you take action too quickly or too soon? Write about a time when non-action was the best defense for achieving the desired outcome.

Write about virtue.

Write about your virtues—the aspects of yourself that are your greatest good. Give a few of these attributes to one of your characters and have him or her use these strengths to avert evil.

Write about a "failure to communicate."

There are times when we have a "failure to communicate." Write about a time when you were completely misunderstood. How did you attempt to rectify the situation? What did you learn from the experience?

Write about a secret.

Write about a secret you have or one that someone told you. What would happen if word got out? What would be the short and long term consequences? Write about the worst-case scenario.

Write about opportunity.

When opportunity knocks, it's best to answer the door. Write about opportunities you have embraced as well as those you have missed or rejected.

Write about a crisis.

Imagine walking through the dark night of the soul. How does the night begin? Where does it end? What do you learn about yourself along the way?

Write about your present situation.

Write about your present situation, the most important thing going on in your life today. What makes it a priority? Who is involved? Are you attached to a specific outcome?

Write about appreciation.

So far, what has been your biggest test and greatest life's lesson? What have you learned to appreciate as a result of this trial? Write about how these circumstances have made you a better person.

JULY

For July, I thought I'd just see what comes up. I happened to be in Seattle taking care of a friend who was recovering from a lung transplant and I'll admit, it wasn't a great experience for me. I managed to find a wonderful yoga class (Yoga to the People) in the University District and I walked on the Burke-Gillman trail as often and as far as time allowed. I thought I'd have ample time to write, but caregiving left me feeling isolated, depleted, and completely uninspired. The day before I left, the prompts for July tumbled out with no particular theme. See where they take your writing.

Write about magic.

Do you believe in magic? If not, why not? If you do, write about the last time something magical happened.

Write about that homeless person.

Write about a homeless person you have seen. Make up their story. Explain how they ended up on the street.

Write about honesty.

If you found $300 at an ATM, would you return it or keep it? How would you justify your actions?

Write about losing something important.

If you lost your ability to hear, what sounds would you miss most? How would you cope with losing your best friend, your partner, your job, your home?

Write about desperation.

Create a character who is desperate enough to kill someone. Put the character in a scene where they decide NOT to do it.

Write about food.

Write about your favorite meal. When did you first taste it? Who were you with? Why is it your favorite?

Write an advice column.

If you were an advice columnist what would you tell someone whose spouse or partner has been unfaithful.

Write about your last year.

If you had a year to live, how would you spend your time? Who would you want to be with? Where would you want to go? What would you say and to whom?

Write about philanthropy.

If you had more money than you needed, what would you do with the excess? What charitable organizations do you support? Why?

Write about gratitude.

Write a letter of gratitude to someone who needs to know how you feel. Send it without expecting anything in return.

Write the truth.

Write a dialogue and scene where you finally tell someone the truth. What is their reaction?

Write about wishes.

If you had three wishes, what would they be? (You can't wish for more wishes). Write about the outcome each wish would provide.

Write a book review.

Write a review of a book you've recently finished reading. Post it on Goodreads. Write about the types of books you enjoy most.

Write about your worst vacation.

Write about your worst vacation. Where did you go? Who was with you? Why was it the worst? What would have made it better?

Write about your best vacation.

Write about your best vacation and what made it the best. Provide lots of details.

Write about something crazy.

Write about a crazy neighbor, friend, relative, or situation. Describe the craziness in detail.

Write about the weather.

Write about your favorite climate, or a severe climate situation paying particular attention to the senses.

Write about your reflection.

Look in the mirror and describe what you see. What is this person thinking and feeling?

Write about forgiveness.

Write a letter where you ask for forgiveness from someone you have wronged. Now, write their response.

Write your "bucket" list.

Make a list of 10 things you want to accomplish before you die. Write about the one you most want.

Write about being stranded.

Imagine being stranded, alone, on an island. Write about your thoughts, feelings, and actions.

Write about animals.

Write about life from your dog, cat, or bird's point of view (POV). If you don't have a pet, write from any animal's POV.

Write about religion or spirituality.

Write about your religious upbringing and how it impacts your life, or about your spiritual practices, your overall belief system and what you think makes the grass grow.

Write about loss.

Write about the most important things in your life. What would you do if they were taken away?

Write about work.

Write about your best and worst jobs or the work you do now. Do you work to live or live to work? Is there balance?

Write about your best friend.

Write about your best friend or your favorite person. What traits do you have in common?

Write a synopsis.

Write a synopsis of a book or short story you have inside of you. Write the first and last sentence of the piece.

Write about your strengths.

Write about why you write. What are your strengths as a writer? What strengths do you have as a person? Contrast your strengths and your weaknesses.

Write about your ideals.

Write about your ideal mate, job, vacation, location and how you go about creating these ideals. If manifesting is difficult, write about that.

Write an entry.

Write a fictitious entry for your community's police blotter or sheriff's log. Or, go to the sheriff's log and pick a situation to write about.

Write a gossip column.

What secrets are you keeping? Change the names to protect the innocent and write about it in detail.

AUGUST

If the quote, "Music is the universal language of mankind," by Henry Wadsworth Longfellow is true, then, no doubt, the titles of songs can be an inspiration to those of us who love to write. This month's prompts are based on a variety of song titles. It doesn't matter if you know the song, all that matters is what memory or situation the title evokes for you. The idea here is to write about whatever comes up in whatever form you choose: poetry, essay, letter, journal entry, short story, memoir, or novel. Read the prompt, take a few deep breaths and write. Whether it's about your deepest thoughts and feelings, your high school crush, or your favorite pet, enjoy the journey.

Write about the song title, *Please Please Me* by The Beatles.

When in your life did you want someone to pay more attention to you or do something to please you? Perhaps the tables are reversed and you are the one who should be more considerate. Maybe this song title by The Beatles inspires something else. Write about whatever comes up.

Write about the song title, *I Can See Clearly Now* by Johnny Nash.

There are times for all of us when we are blind to the truth until something happens to open our eyes. Write about a time in your life when this happened to you, when the fog lifted and you could see a person, situation, or issue clearly.

Write about the song title, *Born to Run* by Bruce Springsteen.

Have you ever felt like you were trapped in a situation that made you want to run away? Maybe you're the type of person who puts down roots and doesn't understand why people leave what appears to be a good situation. Write about whatever the song title means to you.

Write about the song title, *Brain Damage* by Pink Floyd.

Have you ever or are you now doing things that could damage your brain? Are you thinking negative thoughts, consuming too much alcohol or perhaps you abuse yourself in some other way? Maybe you have a friend or family member whose behavior is troubling. Write about whatever *Brain Damage* means to you.

Write about the song title, *You Don't Learn That In School* by The King Cole Trio.

What are some of the biggest lessons you've learned in life? Pick one of the most compelling and write about it. You might want to apply this lesson to a character you're writing about. Or perhaps you want to write about an experience you had in school or something else this song title brings up.

Write about the song title, *Incense and Peppermints* by the Strawberry Alarmclock.

The smell of incense can be overpowering, a strong scent people either love or hate. The same is true with peppermint. Its taste either delights or overwhelms the palate. Is something overpowering you, or are you overpowering to others? Perhaps the song title reminds you of church or a love-in. Whatever it is, just write about it.

Write about the song title, *Five O'Clock World* by The Vogues.

If you have a day job, write about it. What would be your ideal employment situation? Write about the steps you can take to create a better five o'clock world for yourself.

Write about the song title, *Aren't You Glad You're You* by Tiny Tim.

What makes you, you? What traits and attributes set you apart from others? In what ways do you stand out in a crowd? Perhaps you wish you were someone else. Who would that be and why? For fun, create a character based on the most unique and distinctive part of yourself.

Write about the song title, *Toast of The Town* by Motley Crue.

Write about someone who is or who thinks they are the toast of the town. What did they do? How does the recognition they receive make you feel? Do they deserve it? Why or why not? What would you have to do to become the toast of the town? Would you want to be in this enviable position?

Write about the song title, *Fat Lip* by Sum 41.

Have you ever been punched in the face or punched someone? Better yet, have you ever wanted to punch someone but managed to control yourself? If you've ever had a fat lip or wanted to give one to someone, write about the experience that led you to that tipping point. What emotions were you feeling? What were the consequences of your actions?

Write about the song title, *Runaway* by Del Shannon.

Think back to your childhood and write about a time when you wanted to, or actually did, run away. If you never did this, write about a friend or sibling who did. Include reasons why a child wants to run away from home.

Write about the song title, *Respect* by Aretha Franklin.

We all like to be respected, but sometimes we aren't. When was the last time you were disrespected? When was the last time you disrespected someone? Were the actions justified? How did being disrespected make you feel?

Write about the song title, *My Generation* by The Who.

Write about your generation. What makes it unique? Do you fit the stereotype or not? In fifty years, what do you think people will say about your generation? In 100 years, what consequences do you think the inaction, action, or reaction of your generation will have on the global community?

Write about the song title, *A Change is Gonna Come* by Sam Cooke.

Change can be a good thing, but it can also be frightening. What changes are you anticipating and how do they make you feel? What can you do to make the inevitable transition easier or smoother? What conversations do you need to have? What actions do you need to take? Write a scene where two characters work through the situation you are about to face.

Write about the song title, *Stairway to Heaven* by Led Zeppelin.

If there actually was a stairway to heaven, what would it look like and who would greet you at the top? Describe what heaven means to you. Is your heaven here on earth or do you believe you have to die to get there?

Write about the song title, *Superstition* by Stevie Wonder.

Are you superstitious? Do you tremble when a black cat crosses your path or think that walking under a ladder is dangerous? Will a broken mirror result in seven years of bad luck? If you are superstitious, what evidence do you have to support your belief? Write about what superstition means to you.

Write about the song title, *Crazy* by Patsy Cline.

Write about the people, places or things that drive you crazy. Include dialogue between you and the person or object that causes your insanity. Be as outrageous as you can be. This is an opportunity to make crazy funny.

Write about the song title, *Suspicious Minds* by Elvis Presley.

Write about a suspicious character you know about or know personally. This is an opportunity to pretend you are a detective. What clues led you to your belief about this person? Perhaps you're suspicious about your partner or spouse's activities. Write about your suspicions and the consequences should you confront them.

Write about the song title, *You Can't Always Get What You Want* by the Rolling Stones.

Do you believe the song title is true? Do you always get what you want? What do you want that you're not getting? What would your life be like if you finally got it? What steps can you take to get the thing or things you want? Write a scene where you are given that object of your desire. How does it make you feel?

Write about the song title, *Love and Happiness* by Al Green.

Are you in love? Are you happy? If so, write about the things that make you feel this way. If you aren't in love or if you're unhappy, write about the cause and what you plan on doing (if anything) to change the situation. What would it take to bring love and happiness into your life?

Write about the song title, *I Still Haven't Found What I'm Looking for* by U2.

What are you looking for? Are others looking for it too? Why haven't you found it? Are you sure it exists? What will change when you find it? What will happen if you never find it? Will you ever give up and stop looking? Express this situation in a poem.

Write about the song title, *Every Breath You Take* by The Police.

When is the last time something or someone took your breath away? What amazes you most in this life? What could you do to create more moments that take your breath away? Have you ever struggled to breathe? What went through your mind at that time?

Write about the song title, *In the Still of the Night* by The Five Satins.

Continue this story: Jason woke up and looked at the clock. It was 2:00 a.m. and the night was so still, he couldn't hear a sound. Only the sliver of a moon, hanging from the sky let him know his senses were still working. Where was he and how long had he been here?

Write about the song title, *Crying* by Roy Orbison.

What do you have to cry about? When was the last time you cried? What were the circumstances? Were you alone or was someone with you? Maybe you never cry. If this is the case, do you believe not crying impacts your health? Write about the last time you cried or the last time you wanted to cry.

Write about the song title, *The Message* by Grandmaster Flash.

What message is the universe sending you that you are ignoring? What messages are you sending others? How have these messages sealed your fate? Write about a character who ignores an important message and what happens to him or her as a result.

Write about the song title, *Good Vibrations* by The Beach Boys.

Write about a person you know who makes the room light up whenever they enter. If you don't know anyone like that, imagine someone who can do this either literally or metaphorically. Have fun describing a scene involving good vibrations.

Write about the song title, *What's Going On* by Marvin Gaye.

You've been on vacation and come back home to discover a party going on in your living room. You enter the room and no one even notices you. The first words out of your mouth are, "What's going on here?" Write the rest of this scene.

Write about the song title, *Yesterday* by The Beatles.

What did you do yesterday? Did you have fun? Accomplish something important? Do something embarrassing? Write about your day, but from the point of view of your pet. If you don't have a pet, imagine a cat watched your every move.

Write about the song title, *People Get Ready* by the Impressions.

What do you need to get ready to do? Where are you planning to go? What do you wish you were getting ready for? On a more global scale, what should people be getting ready for?

Write about the song title, *Heroes* by David Bowie.

Who is your hero? What role have they played in your life or in the life of a story, poem, or novel you're writing? What makes them unique? Describe this person in detail. What do they look like? How old are they? Where are they from? What specifically do they do that is so heroic?

Write about the song title, *Georgia on My Mind* by Ray Charles.

What have you been thinking about lately? Who or what is on your mind? Do these thought make you feel good or are they upsetting? What are you going to do about it?

SEPTEMBER

September reminds me of back to school, a slight dip in temperature, and harvesting vegetables from the garden. Each year there is an overabundance of something. One year it was tomatoes, another year it was peppers, and this year it's all varieties of squash. While my husband prepares the soil and plants the seeds, I'm in charge of watering and coming up with creative uses for the food we grow. The subject of creativity brings me to the topic of writing prompts for September. Awhile back I stumbled across the book, *Women Know Everything! 3,241 Quips, Quotes & Brilliant Remarks* by Karen Weekes. The book touts "Wit and Wisdom from A to Z." This month's prompts are inspired by the alphabetical organization of the topics.

Write about ability.

We are often judged by our ability or lack of. Write about your strengths and weaknesses. What ability would you like to strengthen? What steps could you take over the next year to become more capable in this area?

Write about acting.

We all enjoy a good play and are often astonished by a strong performance. At the same time, we are often actors in our own personal dramas. Write about a time you acted in a personal drama. Imagine watching yourself on stage. Write a review about your performance.

Write about action.

The difference between success and failure can be as simple as taking action. Write about the results you attained the last time you took action. Then, write about a goal you would like to achieve and the steps required to take action. Now go do it!

Write about activism.

Activism means involvement. Whether you're involved or not, write about a cause that is near and dear to your heart. Include what being active in this cause means to you. If you're not active at the moment, explain why you are not yet taking action and whether you plan to do so in the future.

Write about advertising.

What are your feelings about advertising in general? If you hate advertising, write about a better way to get the word out about products and services. If you enjoy advertising, write about your favorite or most memorable ad.

Write about advice.

Do you love giving advice? Write about your area of expertise and the type of advice you generally offer. Has anyone ever asked you to keep your thoughts and opinions to yourself? Think of someone in your life who could benefit from the advice you have to offer. Instead of telling them what you think, write a letter instead.

Write about age.

Considering your age, how has your life been so far? Write about your most memorable experience or write about something you are looking forward to. What is your attitude about getting older?

Write about alcohol.

If you consume alcohol, write about the first time you experienced the taste. What were you doing? Who were you with? If you've ever gotten drunk, write about that experience. If you abstain from drinking alcohol, write about why you never or no longer drink.

Write about ambition.

There are times in life when we have an enormous drive to accomplish something important. When was the last time you were driven by a desire so strong you knew you could not fail? Write about that time. Perhaps you lack ambition. If so, what is preventing you from reaching your goals?

Write about apathy.

Do you feel apathetic or indifferent about anything? If so, write about what it is and why you feel that way. Is this feeling helping or hurting you? When can apathy be a good thing? If feeling apathetic is thwarting your efforts, write about what you can do to turn this feeling around.

Write about appearance.

Are you guilty of judging a book by its cover or people by their appearance? What does your appearance say about you? Put a chair in front of a mirror and take a careful look at the reflected image. Describe this person (you), imagining you've never seen him or her before. Is this the image you want to project into the world?

Write about art.

Take a notebook and pen and go to a museum (or online) and take a close look at a work of art. It could be a sculpture, oil, watercolor, mixed media, or photograph. Describe the image to someone who is blind. Include the location of the artwork and how looking at the work makes you feel.

Write about beauty.

Describe in detail someone or something you believe is beautiful. What attributes does this person or thing have? If it's a person, does he or she know how you feel about them? Is beauty only skin deep? Is it important?

Write about a bitch.

Think of someone you know who is a bitch and describe them in detail. Then, write some dialogue revealing their bitchy nature. Can you be a bitch and still be likeable? Are there circumstances when being a bitch is a good thing?

Write about your body.

Is your body your temple? Why or why not? What do you do to take care of yourself, or how could you take better care of yourself, or why don't you take care of yourself?

Write about a car.

Write about your first car, your first experience driving, or your first memory of being in a car. What do you think the cars of the future will be like? Do you believe cars will eventually be replaced by other modes of transportation? What would the world be like without cars?

Write about cats.

Do you love or hate cats? Write about a cat you have or had and the role the cat played in your life. If you're not a cat lover, then write a scene where a cat is a villain. Add dialogue between you and the cat.

Write about a challenge.

When was the last time you challenged yourself to do something extraordinary? Describe the situation and the outcome. Perhaps someone challenged you to do something you had never done before. Describe the situation and why you accepted or declined the challenge.

Write about change.

Are you someone who fears change or embraces it? What changes are you afraid to make? Write about the fear that is stopping you. What changes have you recently made? Write about whatever you had to overcome.

Write about children.

How do you feel about children? If you have children of your own, write about the best and worst part of having them. If you don't have children, write about the best and worst part of your childhood. Pick two scenes that come to mind and write out as many details as you can. What can you learn by looking at these situations now that you are older and wiser?

Write about chocolate.

Do you love chocolate? Is it your favorite sweet? If so, write about the first time you had it. If not, write about your favorite dessert. Include the first time you tasted it or who made it, and what it is you love about it.

Write about choices.

In spite of our good intentions, we sometimes end up making choices that we later come to regret. Write about the worst choice you ever made, and then make an effort to find either humor or insight from the situation. Perhaps the bad choice has ultimately made you a better, more compassionate person.

Write about clothes.

Look through your closet and select an article of clothing that represents an important or significant event in your life.

Give this article of clothing a voice of its own and have it "talk" about the event from its point of view.

Write about coffee.

Does coffee play a role in your life? Do you hate it, drink too much of it, or maybe you simply spend time at your local coffee shop? Write about the role coffee plays, doesn't play, or played in your life.

Write about college.

If you went to college, write about the experience and whether it was valuable. If you haven't gone, why not? Write about your opinion of college and whether you believe it's worth the time and money.

Write about communication.

How are your verbal communication skills? Have you ever taken a class to improve your ability to communicate? What difference (if any) did it make in your life?

Write about computers.

How dependent are you on your computer or smart phone? Do you think it's a good idea to unplug every now and then? How long can you go without checking email or surfing the net? Do you have a healthy relationship with computers or does your usage border on addiction or obsession?

Write about confidence.

There are some people who exude confidence and others who obviously lack it. Where are you on the spectrum? What would you do or say if you were more confident in your abilities? Or, write about how your confidence has enabled you to get ahead in the "game."

Write about conflict.

What is one big conflict you have had to deal with or are you presently dealing with? What caused the conflict? Who is involved? What resolution (if any) do you see? Write about the steps you have taken or plan to take to resolve the issue if that is possible.

Write about conformity.

Are you a conformist or nonconformist? Did you follow in your parents' footsteps or carve out your own path? Write about an incident that helped shape your destiny.

OCTOBER

Traditionally, October has been a very significant month. It's the month I moved from Ohio to California, by myself in a 1971 VW, and it's the month I got married. It's also the month where everything in the garden is harvested, the month I make a huge pot of chili and corn bread and invite friends and family for a casual get together, and it's the month for celebrating my favorite holiday, Halloween. For this month, I'm continuing with prompts inspired from Karen Weekes, *Women Know Everything! 3,241 Quips, Quotes & Brilliant Remarks.*

Write about death.

What is your attitude about death? Is it something you fear or does the inevitable end inspire you to live a rich and full life? If you died tomorrow, how would your obituary read? Write the obituary you would like to have.

Write about evil.

Imagine being an evil king or evil queen and write a scene where you wreak havoc on your village. Who would be punished? Who would survive? What motivates your actions?

Write about fame.

Write about someone famous who you admire. Why do you admire this person? What traits, if any, do you share? Is fame something you desire? If so, what steps could you take to become famous? Perhaps you think fame is undesirable. Either way, write about your attitudes about fame.

Write about gossip.

Develop a character who is the town gossip. Describe this character in detail. Include their age and appearance. Pick a location, and create a scene where this person can't hold his tongue. How does the person hearing the gossip react? Have fun with this.

Write about history.

Imagine having the ability to enter a time machine and spend a day, week, or month in a different time and place. Where would you go? What events would you like to witness or be a part of? What role would you assume?

Write about inspiration.

Where do you go or what do you do when you need inspiration? What does it take to build your passion and take your writing or other work to the next level?

Write about jealousy.

Are you a jealous person, or perhaps you live with or have a friend who is jealous? Does your jealousy help you strive to be a better person or does it damage you emotionally? Are there any benefits to being jealous? Is this a character trait you would be better living without?

Write about kissing.

Write about the last person you kissed or who kissed you. Where were you? How long ago was it? How did you feel about the kiss? Did the kiss ignite passion or did it communicate something entirely different?

Write about laughter.

Write about the people or situations that make you laugh. When was the last time you let out a huge belly laugh? How could you bring more laughter into your life? When was the last time you made someone else laugh?

Write about memory.

What is your favorite memory? What is your worst memory? Write about each of them, comparing and contrasting the two situations. What have learned from each of these experiences? Would you change either situation? If so, how?

Write about nature.

Write about your favorite way to spend time in nature or why you don't enjoy spending time in nature. Write about your best or worst-case scenario. If you had an opportunity to climb Mt. Everest (training and Sherpa included) would you do it? Could you do it?

Write about opinions.

We all have opinions, some strong and important, others rather insignificant. Write an essay expressing your opinion about a subject that is important to you. Why is this topic important?

Write about perfection.

Do you strive for perfection or are you more likely to accept the status quo? Is perfection worth the effort or would you be happier and healthier lowering your standards? What do you gain or miss by accepting less than what is considered to be perfect?

Write about a quotation.

Select a quotation that speaks to you and expound upon it. Explain why this quote speaks to you, how it makes you feel, and what you think about the person who said it.

Write about a role model.

Write about someone who is or who was a positive role model for you. What did you learn from this person and how has it been valuable to you. Perhaps you serve as a role model for someone you know. Write about your contributions.

Write about sacrifice.

Write about a time when you had to give up something you valued for some future gain. How did you feel at the time? How do you feel now, looking back? Was your action at the time worth the sacrifice or would you do things differently knowing what you know now?

Write about temptation.

What is your greatest temptation? How often do you give in? What are the consequences for your actions? Write about any attempts you have made to avoid this temptation and whether it worked for you. If you always give in, write about why you don't or can't stop.

Write about ugly.

Write about whatever the word, ugly, means to you. Perhaps it pertains to someone you know, a building in your neighborhood, a beloved pet, or your thoughts.

Write about violence.

Have you ever been involved in a violent situation? If so, describe the event, how you felt at the time, and how you feel now. Is violence ever justified? If you are currently experiencing violence, what steps can you take to change the situation?

Write about writing better.

Why do you write? What are you currently writing? What do you wish you could write? Make a list of things you can do to improve your writing skills or reach your goals as a writer.

Write about an X-Ray.

Write about a time when you have suffered an injury and needed an X-Ray. What caused you to get hurt? What activities did you need to stop doing during your recover? If you've never had an X-Ray, perhaps you're overly cautious or unadventurous.

Write about youth.

If you are still young, write about the benefits and the disadvantages of your age. If you are "of a certain age," compare your youth to who you have become. Are you older? Wiser? Happier? Is your life going the way you imagined it would? Do you believe George Bernard Shaw was right when he said, "Youth is wasted on the young?"

Write about depression.

Have you ever been depressed or known someone who suffered from depression? What was the root cause? Create a character sketch for someone who is hopelessly depressed then create a scene that gives them hope.

Write about education.

Has your education served you or are there gaps that need to be filled? What online classes could you take or books could you read to fill those gaps? What is your opinion of education in America? How could it be better?

Write about kindness.

Imagine that it is your job to perform random acts of kindness without being identified. Make a list of ten things you would do. Write a flash fiction (300-1000 words) story where the character has this job.

Write about silence.

Create a scene where the main character reveals something important about his character without saying a word. As an alternative, write a scene from your life where you were silent or silence was (or would have been) the best option.

Write about intuition.

Write a scene (based on fact or fiction) where a character's intuition saves him. When was the last time you followed your intuition or should have followed it? What role has intuition played in your life, if any?

Write about government.

Do you believe our government is doing its job? Do you believe people need more rules? What policies would you change if you were in charge of the country? If you have something important to say, take time now to write a letter to your Congressman.

Write about relationships.

Write about the best and worst relationships you have ever had. What made them good or bad? Write a self-help column (or a song) advising someone who needs to leave a bad relationship and doesn't know how.

Write about heart versus head.

Imagine your car breaks down in a remote area that has no cell reception. Write a scene about the situation using your head. Write it again using your heart. Which scene do you like better? Why?

Write about Halloween.

Write about your most memorable Halloween. If Halloween isn't remarkable, write about holidays in general—the one you like best or the one you wish would just go away.

NOVEMBER

This month I'm going to India. It's a tour with 30 others from around the U.S. and Canada. The itinerary is full of tourist stops and sightseeing, and we will be covering a lot of ground in a very short time (2 weeks). In preparation for the tour I've been thinking about topics that would be interesting to write about—whether you're traveling halfway around the world or going on a weekend adventure. This month's prompts are designed to encourage you to notice the people, places, and things near and far, and become a keen observer of your environment.

Write about travel.

Is travel important to you? Did your family travel when you were a child? Where did you go? If you didn't travel as a child, where did you want to go?

Write about where you want to go.

If you could go anywhere in the world, where would you go? What would be the primary purpose of your trip? What's stopping you? What can you do to make travel a part of your future?

Write about indispensable items.

Whether you're going on an overnight trip or planning to spend a month away, what items do you always take with you? What items are indispensable and why are they so important?

Write about activities.

What do you enjoy most when you vacation? Shopping? Fine dining? Talking to locals? Hanging out at the beach? Visiting museums, art galleries and churches? Write about your favorite things to do when you're on vacation.

Write about being alone or in a group.

Do you prefer traveling alone or in groups? Write about the advantages and disadvantages of both. Be sure to use examples if you have them.

Write about a destination.

Research a place you might like to go (it might even be your home town), then write an 800-word article listing the top 10 reasons to visit this particular place.

Write about your curiosity.

Write a list of questions that you would like to ask locals (politicians, teachers, students, etc.) in the area where you are going. Try to get all of them answered by the end of your trip.

Write about a place.

Go to a restaurant or coffeehouse you've never been to before. Describe the employees and customers you see. What are they wearing? Are they in a hurry or taking their time? What are they talking about?

Write about sounds.

Go outside, close your eyes, and spend some time listening. Write about the sounds you hear. Try describing the concert of sounds with your words.

Write about smell.

Imagine that you are Helen Keller. Describe a location using only your sense of smell. Is this even possible?

Write about a cultural event.

Write about a cultural event that takes place in your home town or in a place you are visiting. What is the purpose of this event? What is the history? Who is attending? How does being at the event make you feel?

Write about an historical landmark.

Observe an historical landmark and describe it in detail. What is it made of? How big is it? Why was it erected? Who or what does it honor?

Write about transportation.

Go to a populated area and describe the various modes of transportation. How do most people get around? Were you surprised by anything you see?

Write about food.

What foods are unique to the area where you live or where you are going? Find and/or make a local recipe and write about it.

Write about someone famous (or infamous).

What famous (or infamous) people live or have lived in the area you are visiting? Imagine having a conversation with one of them. Write the dialogue.

Write about the weather.

What season is it? What's the temperature? What special clothing do you need to protect yourself from the elements? Do you enjoy this type of climate or not? Why?

Write about accommodations.

Where are you staying? Describe your accommodations. Do they meet or exceed your expectations? Are they disappointing? What amenities surprised you? Was there enough hot water? Did you know how to use the toilets?

Write about your traveling companions.

Write about one or more of your traveling companions. If you're traveling alone, write about someone you met along the way. Are you a good match or do they drive you crazy?

Write about the flora and fauna.

Write about the flora and fauna of the area, or something in nature that is remarkable or that you've never seen before. Compare this location to one where you usually spend your time.

Write about art.

Look for some unique handcrafted items and write about the art and the artists. What makes these items unique? Did you buy anything you saw? Why or why not?

Write about clothing.

What type of clothing do most people wear in the town or country you are visiting? Think about style, texture, and color. In what other ways do people in this location adorn themselves?

Write about customs.

What is the predominant religion or custom of the place you are visiting? If possible, attend a religious service that is different from your faith and write about it. If you can't attend a service, try to interview a member of the congregation and write about what you've learned.

Write about the bizarre and unusual.

Write about the most bizarre or unusual thing you have observed or experienced during your trip. Where were you? How did this make you feel?

Write about comfort.

How does being in this town or country make you feel? Are you "a fish out of water" or does it feel like home? Would you return? Why or why not?

Write about beauty.

Describe something beautiful without saying what it is. It could be a person, a sound, a place, or a thing. Use your imagination. Perhaps, write a poem.

Write about the locals.

Describe some of the locals you have met. Are they friendly and helpful or do they appear to be disinterested in you? Pick someone and imagine walking in their shoes, then write about their day.

Write about a newspaper headline.

What are today's newspaper headlines? If they aren't in your language, ask someone to translate. Write a news story based on what you know.

Write about the best.

Write 500-800 words about the best part of your trip. Why was this the best part? Were you alone or with others?

Write about the worst.

Write 500-800 words about an aspect of the trip you could have lived without. If possible, find humor in the situation—even though it might not have been funny at the time.

Write about your photos.

If you have photos from your travels, pick out your five favorites. Write captions and a 300-word paragraph about each of them. Share them with your friends and/or family.

DECEMBER

As the last month of the year, December is a good time to evaluate the past eleven months and set intentions for the coming year. By taking time to reflect on our goals, accomplishments, and challenges, we can make sense of the past and perhaps move forward with more confidence and direction. December is also a good time to take stock of our attitudes and beliefs, identifying those that serve us and those that benefit from a rewrite. This type of evaluation can also extend to our friendships, work situations and lifestyles. The prompts for this month are designed to get you to think about what has been working for you, and where you might want to rewrite your history and perhaps your destiny.

Write about something significant.

What was the most significant event that occurred this past year? Was it something you planned or was it unexpected? How did it make you feel? Were others involved? Write about it in detail.

Write about an expensive purchase.

Write about something you bought that was somewhat extravagant. In hindsight, was it worth the money? Perhaps you didn't buy something you really wanted or needed. In either case, write your internal dialogue. Include any insight you now have into your attitude about money.

Write about an embarrassing moment.

This could be something that happened to you or to someone else. It might even be something you read or heard about. Do you ever not do something because you might be embarrassed by the outcome? Write a scene (real or imagined) where you or your character is completely embarrassed, but somehow recovers.

Write about your inner-most desire.

Identify your deepest desire and write about it as if it is a reality. Use first person, present tense, and as much detail as you can, including all of the senses.

Write about disappointment.

Looking back at the past year, what has been your biggest disappointment? What if anything could you have done to avoid being or feeling let down? What lesson did you learn from this experience?

Write about a dream.

It could be a something you hope will happen in the future or something you remember during sleep. Do you believe dreams can come true or that they can be premonitions of things to come? Think of a challenge in your life and write a dream that holds a solution.

Write about change.

If you were the ruler of the universe, what one thing would you change? How would this make the world a better place?

How would this affect your friends, family and community? Perhaps you have experienced a difficult transition or would like to change something about yourself. Write about what the word change means to you.

Write about an accomplishment.

Write about something you would like to accomplish this coming year and the steps you will take to make this desire a reality. Explain why this is important to you.

Write about family.

Think about your family and those you love. Write about their importance in your life and what you can do this coming year to express your feelings of gratitude and appreciation towards them.

Write about the holiday season.

Some people love the holidays and others dread the season. Write about how the holiday season makes you feel. Are there traditions you cherish or does all the hoop-la make you uncomfortable? Write about where you believe the source of your current attitude comes from.

Write about your home.

Where do you live? What does your home or apartment look like? Who lives with you (include pets)? Include the surrounding environment as well as the emotional climate.

Write about your health.

Stand in front of a full-length mirror and write about the person you see. How does his appearance compare to how he feels? Does he need to eat better? Exercise more? Develop healthy habits? Pretend this person is a stranger and write a prescription for a better life.

Write about learning.

What would you like to learn or be better at this coming year? How will you gain this knowledge? Write a plan for accomplishing this educational goal. Include the tools you will need, the cost, and the start date.

Write about clutter.

What is cluttering up your life or your personal space? Perhaps you know someone who is a hoarder. Write an essay about hoarding. Be sure to include solutions.

Write about your pets.

If you don't have pets of your own, write about your neighbor's pet or the one you wish you had. What value do pets have in people's lives? What would your pets say to you if they could talk?

Write about your destiny?

What were you put on earth to do? Write a scene where your destiny is fulfilled. Include details: age, location, steps taken, and how attaining your destiny makes you feel.

Write about adventure.

Write about an adventure you have taken or one you would like to take. Where did you go? What did you do? Who were you with? What did it cost? What adventure do you have planned for the coming year?

Write about a chance encounter.

Have you ever had a chance encounter that has changed your life? If so, write about it in detail. If this has never happened to you, imagine an encounter that could be life-changing and write about that.

Write about music.

Is there enough music in your life? What music do you listen to? When was the last time you saw a live concert? Write about how music makes you feel and how you can bring more music into your life.

Write about sports.

What sports have you played, do you currently play, or enjoy as a spectator? What sports would you like to play? Write about sports and how they fit (or don't fit) into your life.

Write about your beliefs.

Are you holding on to certain beliefs that prevent you from moving forward in your life? Write about the religious or moral beliefs that prevent you from doing something you want to do, but believe is wrong. Create a scene with a character who does not have such beliefs.

Write about admiration.

Who do you admire? What qualities and traits does he or she have that inspire you? Write about the qualities you have in common and what you could do to be more like him or her.

Write about the coming year.

Write about how you would you like your life to be this coming year. What goals would you like to accomplish? What goal is most important to you? What steps will you take to make sure you accomplish this objective?

Write about the future.

Write about the person you will be in five, ten, and fifteen years from now. What would your family and friends say about you? Imagine interviewing them now and in the future, and write their responses to various interview questions.

Write about grace.

Is there a situation you are dealing with or have dealt with that requires or could have benefited from a more graceful approach? Is this an attribute you have or would like to acquire? Write about how grace could help overcome a difficult or frustrating situation or person.

Write about resources.

What resources do you possess that make a positive difference in your life? Consider friends, family, career, as well as personal attributes. If your resources are limited, write about what you can do to acquire more.

Write about excitement.

What are you excited about? What activity or event are you looking forward to? What book can't you put down? Maybe it's food or a restaurant that gets your juices flowing. Whatever it is, describe it in detail.

Write about hindsight.

Knowing what you know now, what could you have done differently? Write the scene the way it was and the way it "coulda, shoulda, woulda" been.

Write about happiness.

Do you believe that happiness is our birthright? Who deserves to be happy and at what price? Write about a time you sacrificed your happiness for someone else's. Was it worth it?

Write about sacrifice.

What if anything are you willing to sacrifice to reach your goals this coming year? What have you sacrificed to get where you are today? Was it worth the price?

Write about what is sacred.

What do you hold sacred, and why is this so important to you? Was there an incident that caused you to feel this way? In what ways is your life blessed?

The End.

www.ingramcontent.com/pod-product-compliance
Lightning Source LLC
Chambersburg PA
CBHW071312040426
42444CB00009B/1985